Logic Fun

by Michele Best Jackson

illustrated by Tony Waters

cover design by Jeff Van Kanegan

Publisher
Instructional Fair · TS Denison
Grand Rapids, Michigan 49544

About the Author

Michele Best Jackson lives in Tucson, Arizona, with her husband, Roger, and their two toddlers, Laura and Kyle. She received a BA from the University of Arizona. Michele has taught grades 2-8. and currently coordinates and teaches the gifted program, C.A.T.S., for the Flowing Wells Unified School District in Tucson. This is Michele's third published activity book on logic. When Michele isn't writing or teaching, she enjoys beach camping, snorkeling, cooking, and playing with her children.

ISBN: 1-56822-467-2
Logic Fun
Copyright © 1997 by Instructional Fair • TS Denison
2400 Turner Avenue NW
Grand Rapids, Michigan 49544

Table of Contents

About This Book

The puzzles in this book were developed to help students improve some thinking skills while having fun at the same time. The critical thinking skills practiced include the following: gathering and organizing information, comparing facts, deductive reasoning, math logic, and working backwards. The problems are also designed to help individuals practice the patience and perseverance involved in a problem-solving situation.

The book contains four different types of puzzles. The puzzles of each type increase with difficulty as the book progresses. For three of the puzzle types, there is a page of explanation that will help you to develop a strategy for solving that particular type of puzzle. One type of puzzle does not have this option because there are many different avenues you may choose to solve the problems.

The main purpose of this book is to provide fun and challenging puzzles that will help you to polish critical thinking and problem-solving skills. The puzzles are enjoyable to work and provide an excellent opportunity for experimentation with logic in a nonthreatening, non-graded situation.

Say What?

One of the first things you should practice before trying to solve a logic puzzle is how to derive information from the wacky sentences that act as clues to a puzzle. This page will give you some examples and help you polish those skills. The sentences below do not solve a specific puzzle; they are just to get your thinking started.

Step 1. Before attempting a puzzle, read every statement or sentence carefully.

Step 2. Look at the grid or the picture involved to help you clarify what you are doing in a particular puzzle.

Step 3. After rereading a statement, list a fact that is not a possibility based on that particular statement.

Example: Statement: Roger is friends with the parrot owner. You deduce: Roger must not be the parrot owner.

Step 4. When possible, reread a statement and list a fact that is a possibility based on that particular statement.

Example: Statement: Three teachers had salad and one had soup. Mrs. Shulte is allergic to lettuce. You deduce: Mrs. Shulte must have had the soup.

Step 5. Double check your statements carefully, listing all the facts that are and are not possibilities, one at a time, until all are listed. Often there are several facts within one statement. See the example below:

Example:
Statement: Carla went with Smith and the youngest sister to see the lacrosse player.
Facts:
Carla is not Smith.
Carla is not the youngest sister.
Carla is not the lacrosse player.
Smith is not the youngest sister.
Smith is not the lacrosse player.
The youngest sister is not the lacrosse player.

Step 6. This is probably the most important of all...remind yourself not to get overwhelmed by the information. Read the information slowly and remember you can deduce only one fact at a time. YOU CAN DO IT!

Fruit Salad

Introduction: This page is not a puzzle; it is a practice page for you to use so you can polish your deductive reasoning before attempting puzzles.

1. Elizabeth sat next to the girl who brought pineapple.

   Deduce: _Elizabeth did not bring pineapple_

2. Carrie is older than McKethen and the girl who brought Kiwi.

   Deduce:
   1. _Carrie is not the girl who brought Kiwi_
   2. _Carrie is not McKethen_
   3. _The Kiwi girl is not the oldest_
   4. _McKethen is not the oldest_
   5. _Carrie is not the youngest_

3. Barnes is older than the one who brought the banana but younger than his uncle who brought watermelon.

   Deduce:
   1. _Barnes did not bring the banana_
   2. _The Uncle is the oldest_
   3. _Barnes did not bring watermelon_
   4. _Barnes is not the oldest_
   5. _Bananas is not the oldest_

BAR   BAN   UNC
12   14   13

Winter Wonderland

The Zona family spent the day at Winter Park yesterday. They had a real cool time. You can play with the facts below and use the grid to figure out how each of them spent their time.

1. Look at the grid. Notice that there are four family members and 4 different activities. Each person did one activity.

2. Anthony is the ice skater's dad. This means that Anthony is not the _____. Place an X in the Anthony ice skater box.

3. Beth is mother to the ice skater and the sledder. This statements tells us that Beth was not the _____ or the _____. Place an X in those boxes. Now you know that Beth did one of these two activities: _____ or _____.

4. Josh's and Beth's activities required hills. Think about this. Which two activities required hills? Answer: _____ and _____. We already know that Beth did not go sledding so Beth must have been the one to go _____. Now you can place a star in the box that correlates to Beth and skiing. This also tells you that Beth did not build a snowman so you may place an X in that box. Also, if you know that Beth went skiing then you may put an X in the skiing boxes of Josh, Damian, and Anthony.

5. Now, back to the last clue...if Josh's activity also required a hill then Josh must have done what? _____ Now, place a star or a smiley face in that box. This also means that Josh didn't build a snowman or go ice skating. You should now be able to finish the puzzle on your own. Have fun and stay cool!

	Skiing	Snowman	Ice Skating	Sledding
Beth				
Josh				
Damien				
Anthony				

Bagel Bakery

Every Friday morning, the Clifton family started the weekend with a bagel breakfast. Roll around with the facts below to see what kind of bagels Darryl, Tammy, Jennifer, and Josh, the dog, each ate last Friday.

Facts:
1. Tammy's favorite is onion and Darryl's favorite is garlic. Unfortunately, neither of them got their favorite last Friday.
2. Darryl ate his bagel after the sesame and onion bagels were already eaten.
3. The dog and Tammy ate their bagels before Darryl ate his, but Jennifer ate her bagel last.

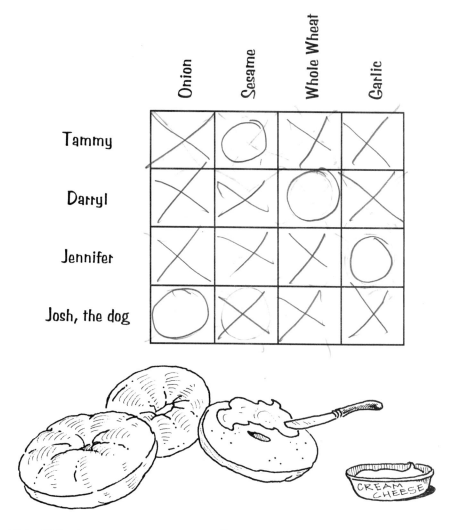

Bottoms Up!

Four friends decided to make upside-down cakes for the church bazaar. Each decided to make a different kind of cake, but all the cakes would be served upside down. Stir your brain up a bit and figure out which friend made which kind of upside-down cake!

Facts:

1. Minnie's cake had pineapple, while Sue's did not.
2. Jean's and Minnie's cakes had the word *apple* in the names, and each of them had only one topping on their cakes.

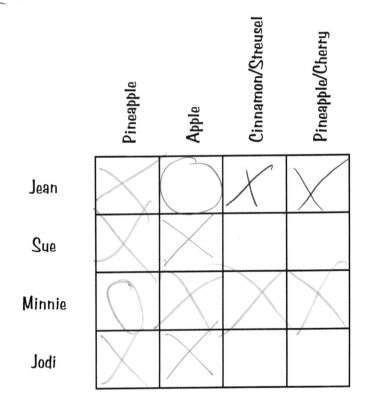

	Pineapple	Apple	Cinnamon/Streusel	Pineapple/Cherry
Jean	X	O	X	X
Sue	X	X		
Minnie	O	X	X	X
Jodi	X	X		

Rollin', Rollin', Rollin'

Last Saturday, the Markzon family decided to get their family exercise a bit differently. Instead of walking, they decided they should be rolling. Wheel through the facts and figure out how each person rolled around the neighborhood.

Facts:

1. Neither Heide nor Seth had the lowest number of wheels or the highest number of wheels.
2. Seth had one more wheel than Andrea.
3. Jason liked his wheels the most because he could use them in his neighborhood or at a rink.
4. Andrea needed excellent balance to ride her cycle.

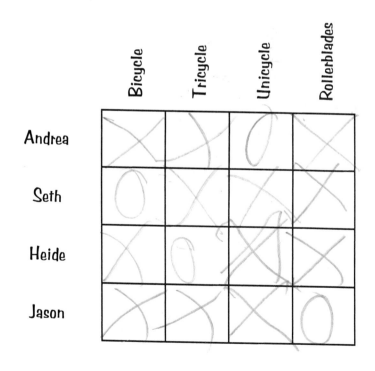

Shell Seekers

The Clinkingbeard family went looking for shells during their last visit to the beach. Out of respect for conservation, each family member agreed to take only one shell. Sift through these sandy facts and deduce who found what type of shell.

Facts:
1. Caleb looked for a cone shell but never found one.
2. Lucas found his shell at the same location where the oyster shell was found.
3. Kandy was excited when Josh found a razor clam.
4. Caleb and Randy's shells start with the same letter.

	Conch	Cone	Razor	Oyster	Mollusk
Joshua	X	X	O	X	X
Caleb	O	X	X	X	X
Kandy	X	X	X	X	O
Lucas	X	X	X	O	X
Randy	X	O	X	X	X

Top Dogs

Six brothers and a sister made hot dogs for lunch yesterday. Each one prefers his/her hot dog a certain way. Munch through the facts to deduce how the siblings topped their dogs. Be smart! Some people had more than one topping!

Facts:
1. Samuel loves ketchup on hamburgers but not on hot dogs.
2. Matthew does not like mustard, and Betty and Samuel love onions.
3. Bob, Matthew, and Derrick each had only one topping on their hot dogs.
4. Derrick does not like ketchup or mustard.

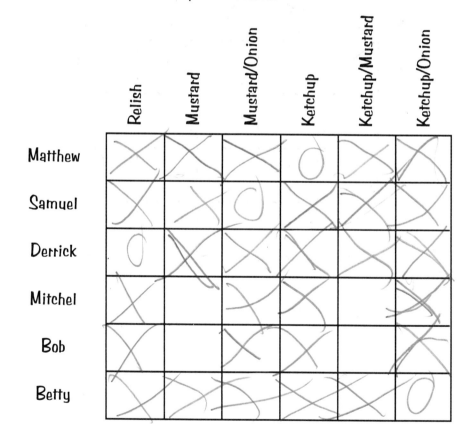

Goosebumps

Mary and Papa Lou from Granbury, Texas, have seven grandchildren, two boys and five girls. The last time they gathered, there was a terrible storm and they lost electricity. They passed the time by confessing what kinds of things give each of them goosebumps. Creep and crawl through these facts, and you will also know what gives them the chills.

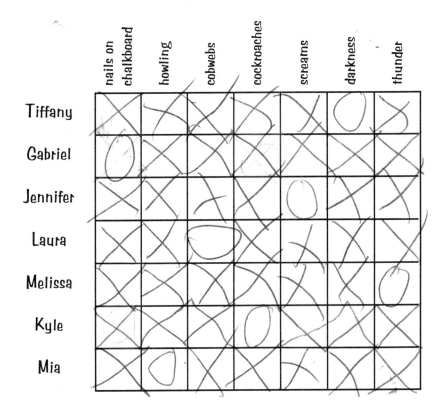

Facts:
1. Kyle and Laura are brother and sister.
2. Jennifer, Mia, and Melissa are all afraid of some type of noise.
3. Laura and her brother are both afraid of something to do with "bugs."
4. The boys get goosebumps from cockroaches and nails on a chalkboard.
5. Mia is not afraid of thunder; Jennifer is afraid of a human-made noise.

Fraction Action

Last week Mr. Tompkins gave a math quiz. Four of the top students scored 95 percent, each missing 1 of 20. Put your logic to work and figure out which student missed each problem; you need to find the fraction each one missed and its equivalent decimal.

	1/8	7/20	3/8	4/15	.375	.26	.35	.125
Joanna								
Alex								
David								
Lydian								

Facts:

1. Joanna and Alex missed the problems with the same denominator.
2. Alex and Joanna had the largest and the smallest decimals. (Be careful with this one; be smart about decimals!)
3. David and Lydian each missed a problem with two decimal places.
4. Alex and Lydian missed the problems with the largest and the smallest numerators.

No Way, José

Poor José. Poor, poor José. All he wanted to do was borrow something to play with from one of his brothers or sisters. But every time he asked to borrow something, each of them shouted, "NO WAY, JOSÉ!" When you solve this sad logic puzzle, you will know which brothers and sisters would not let him borrow their toys and which toys they refused to share. Oh yeah, could you please pass the Kleenex?

Facts:
1. The rollerblade owner has two digits in his/her age.
2. Ramon is one year younger than the sister who owns the soccer ball.
3. Manny is older than Isela but younger than the one who has a stick.

	12 years	9 years	15 years	10 years	Rollerblades	Pogo stick	Soccer ball	Bicycle
Isela								
Carolina								
Rámon								
Manny								
Rollerblades		✕		
Pogo stick				
Soccer ball				
Bicycle				

We Be Jammin'

These brown baggers never eat lunch in the cafeteria. They cannot go through a day without their peanut butter and jelly sandwiches. Spread out the logic here as you munch through the facts to deduce who likes what kind of "jam" on peanut butter and which type of bread each prefers.

Facts:
1. Sara and the wheat-berry eater are cousins to the marmalade lover and Brandon.
2. Jesse does not like apples or strawberries, but he loves wheat bread.
3. Christina and the croissant eater love apples.
4. The strawberry eater likes crushed wheat bread.
5. Grapes are favored by the croissant eater and Brandon.
6. Brandon, Christina, and the apple/grape eater do not like any kind of wheat bread.
7. Christina does not like sourdough, but Nick likes wheat-berry bread.

	Whole Wheat	Wheat-berry	Crushed wheat	White	Sourdough	Croissant	Raspberry	Marmalade	Grape	Apple	Apple/Grape	Strawberry
Keegan												
Brandon												
Jesse												
Christina												
Nick												
Sara												
Raspberry												
Marmalade												
Grape												
Apple												
Apple/Grape												
Strawberry												

Church Camp

Have you ever been to church camp? Well, these girls have been, and they had a blast! When you have solved this puzzle, you will know which girls stayed in which cabins, what city each called home, and their favorite free-time activities while at camp. Have fun.

	Cabin 3	Cabin 3	Cabin 4	Cabin 4	Sacramento	Salt Lake City	San Diego	Sante Fe	Pottery	Baskets	Watercolor	Quilting
Nicole												
Jessica												
Sara												
Kusuma												
Pottery								
Baskets								
Watercolor								
Quilting								
Sacramento				
Salt Lake City				
San Diego				
Sante Fe				

Facts:
1. The girls from California did not room together.
2. The girls in cabin #3 were from New Mexico and California. One made baskets while the other did pottery.
3. Kusuma went to cabin #4 to see Nicole's quilt; she could not believe she and Kusuma were from the same state.
4. Jessica and her roommate from San Diego went to cabin # 3 to see Sara's basket.

Cheese, Please

These six students from Mrs. Jackson's class just love cheese. See if you can slice through the statements and find enough facts to help you solve this puzzle. When you have completed this grid, you should know which student liked which type of cheese and each person's favorite thing to eat with the cheese.

Facts:
1. Amber and Eric both love cheese that starts with a P.
2. The students who eat the hamburger and the hot dog eat cheddar and muenster cheese.
3. The fruit and the "vegetable" were eaten by Sam and the pepper-cheese fan.
4. Brianna and the provolone eater both ate their cheese on a "bread" item.
5. Eric is good friends with the pepper-cheese eater and the bagel lover.
6. The muenster eater, hamburger eater, and Sam are all brothers.
7. The apple eater, the brie cheese lover, and Amber all live on the same street.
8. Ryan does not care for muenster cheese.

	Hot dog	Bagel	Cracker	Tomato	Apple	Hamburger	Amber	Elvis	Ryan	Brianna	Eric	Sam
Cheddar												
Jack												
Pepper												
Provolone												
Brie												
Muenster												
Amber												
Elvis												
Ryan												
Brianna												
Eric												
Sam												

Hang On, Harry!

Harry Hildenbocker has an awesome but hair-raising job. He travels around the United States and rides roller coasters and other similar rides and writes reviews about them for newspapers and magazines. In the puzzle below, you will learn about three of his favorites. After looping through these statements, you will know the following about each ride: the name, the state in which it is located, its top speed, its highest elevation, and its longest drop. Be careful when solving this one; it's easy to confuse the height and the drop measurements.

Facts:

1. The ride in Ohio and the one that drops 131 feet both start with an "m."

2. The Montu has a top speed which is 1 mile per hour more than the ride that has a high elevation of 145 feet, but the Montu is slower than the ride in California.

3. The Mantis has a drop that is longer than the ride in Florida but not as long as the ride which has an elevation of 415 feet.

4. The Superman drops from its point of highest elevation.

	highest elevation					top speed			longest drop		
	Ohio	Florida	California	415 feet	145 feet	132.6 feet	60 mph	100 mph	61 mph	131 feet	137 feet	415 feet
Montu												
Mantis												
Superman												
131 feet												
137 feet												
415 feet												
60 mph												
100 mph												
61 mph												
415 feet												
145 feet												
132.6 feet												

longest drop

top speed

highest elevation

The Pancake Mistake

Oh man! Have you ever eaten so much that you felt like you were about to burst? Well, that is how the Ptasnik family felt after participating in their annual church pancake-eating contest. After you chew through these statements, you will be able to explain who ate which kind of pancake, how many pancakes he or she ate, and the age of each participant.

Facts:

1. Annie ate more pancakes than Luna but fewer than Daniel.
2. Luna and the other teenager, Michael, both had fruit in their pancakes. One of them won the contest, and one came in last place with a stomachache.
3. The pecan pancake eater ate his age in pancakes.
4. Daniel and the banana-nut pancake eater are cousins of the 12-year old and the blueberry lover.
5. Michael is younger than Daniel, but he ate more pancakes than Daniel.
6. Luna is exactly one year younger than the banana-nut pancake eater.
7. Annie and the person who ate exactly one less pancake than she did both had cinnamon in their cakes.
8. Niko is the youngest, and Annie loves fruit in her pancakes.

	Apple cinnamon	Pecan	Banana Nut	Blueberry	Cinnamon	21 years	8 years	16 years	15 years	12 years	23 pancakes	21 pancakes	19 pancakes	18 pancakes	14 pancakes
Daniel															
Annie															
Luna															
Niko															
Michael															
23 pancakes															
21 pancakes															
19 pancakes															
18 pancakes															
14 pancakes															
21 years															
8 years															
16 years															
15 years															
12 years															

Time Out!

Renate, John, Eric, Debbie, Manny, and Linda are all elementary school principals. Unfortunately, part of a principal's job has to do with putting students in "time out" for inappropriate behavior. Some days things are so hectic they feel like pulling their hair out, but they always return the next day with a smile. They relax and get refocused by taking their own "time out." Use the statements below to deduce their first and last names and what they do when they need "time out."

Facts:
1. Eric and Mr. Black went to college with the "divers."
2. Mrs. Schreiner and Renate both took time out by jumping into thin air.
3. The water sports were enjoyed by John and Mr. Valenzuela
4. The skydiver, Renate, and _____ Jehle are all females.
5. Mr. Black and Mr. Valenzuela always eat breakfast with the rollerblader and Debbie.
6. Mr. Abrahms, Linda, and the skydiver live on the same street.
7. Eric, Mr. Valenzuela, and the rollerblader are big Kansas University fans.

	Black	Schreiner	Valenzuela	Jehle	Abrahms	Krompasky	Renate	John	Manny	Debbie	Linda	Eric
Go carts												
Rollerblades												
Bungee jumping												
Water slides												
Skydiving												
Scuba diving												
Renate												
John												
Manny												
Debbie												
Linda												
Eric												

Bats Are Where It's At

Kamron recently did a fabulous report on bats found in North America. You will find illustrations of four bats below. Fly through these facts to identify each bat.

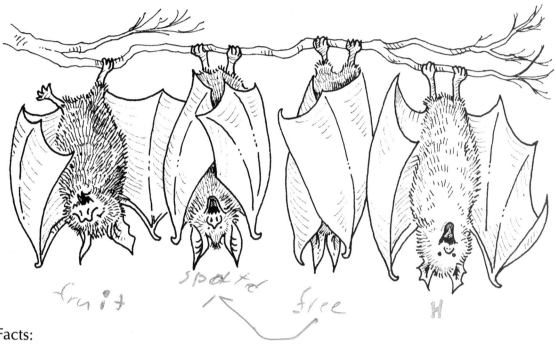

fruit   spotted   free   H

Facts:

1. The spotted bat is between the freetail and the hoary bat. (Does this clue help you at this time? If not, move to #2 and come back to this later.)

2. In this illustration, the fruit bat and the hoary bat each have only one bat next to them. (Now you know that the fruit bat and the hoary bat must be on each end. Label each end bat with both names and later you can eliminate the names you deduce are not correct.)

3. The freetail bat is somewhere to the left of the hoary bat. (Take a very close look at where you think the hoary bat might be. Consider both possibilities.)

4. Go back to clue number one, start again, and solve the puzzle.

Summer Snooze

After a hard day of playing frisbee golf and chasing waves, four buddies, Greg, Mark, Skipper, and Sam, decided to take a summer snooze. Sift through the two facts below and label each hammock with the appropriate snoozer.

Facts:
1. Neither Mark nor Skipper was on either end, but Mark was closer to Greg.
2. From this point of view, Sam is to the right of Skipper.

Jeepers Creepers! Where'd You Get Those Peepers?

Take a close look at these facts and determine who is wearing these wacky sunglasses. The girls' names are Helen, Allyson, Natasha, Shawna, and Kimberly.

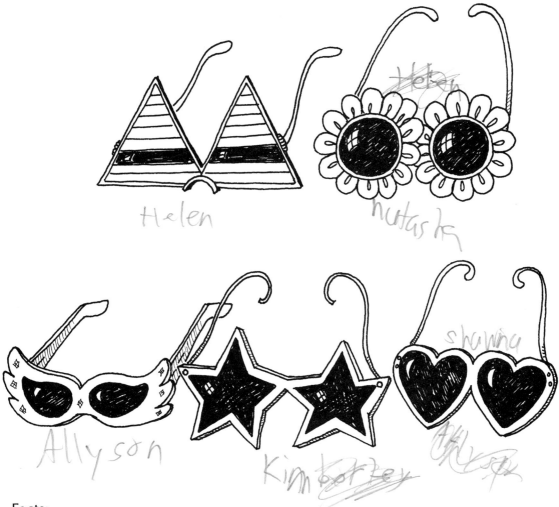

Helen

natasha

Allyson

Kimberley

shawna

Facts:
1. Natasha is behind and between Kimberly and Shawna.
2. From Kimberly's point of view, Allyson is to her direct right.
3. Helen is behind Allyson and the girl wearing star-shaped glasses.

Totally Tubular

The Lehman family enjoyed a visit to the Big Wave Water Park last Sunday after church. Their favorite ride was one called Tubers. Mr. and Mrs. Lehman stood at the bottom of the ride trying *to* figure out which of their kids was in each tube. All they could see were arms and legs; their kids were whooshing down the slide inside foam tubes. Splash around with these facts and see if you can figure out where Danny, Ben, Jessa, Debbie, and Kila are.

Facts:
1. Neither Danny nor Kila is in the exact middle.
2. Debbie and Danny are next to each other. Ben is not next to Jessa.
3. Ben is between Danny and Kila.
4. Debbie is directly behind Danny, and Jessa is directly in front of Kila.
5. Jessa isn't close to the end of the line.

Windy 500

Have you ever heard of the Indy 500? Well, of course, you have! Have you ever heard of the Windy 500? It is a kite height race. The person who gets his or her kite to a height of 500 feet wins a $50 gift certificate good at the local hobby store. Your job is to fly through these statements and deduce how each kite is decorated. When you have completed the puzzle, please decorate the kites and do not be afraid to be creative.

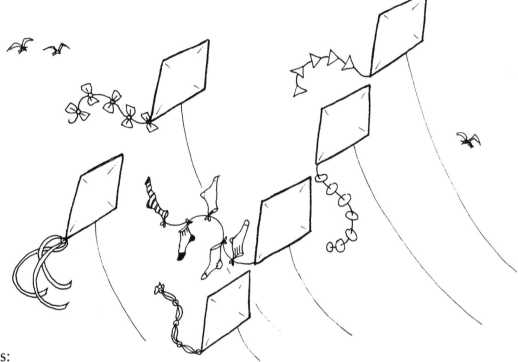

Facts:

1. There are six kites. They are decorated as follows: a rainbow, a fish, polka-dotted, stars and stripes, solid green, and solid purple.
2. Neither of the solid-colored kites won the race, and they are not side by side, nor are they directly behind each other.
3. The polka-dotted kite is higher than the green kite but below the stars and stripes kite.
4. The stars and stripes kite and the purple kite are higher than the rainbow and the green kite.
5. The stars and stripes kite and the fish kite are at the lowest and highest elevations.
6. The rainbow kite is directly above the fish kite.

Heads Up, Seven Up

During a recent benefit for disabled veterans, seven paratroopers from an Air Force base in Texas decided to show their stuff. They used their most colorful parachutes to put on quite a show. There were seven different colors of parachutes: purple, blue, green, orange, turquoise, red, and yellow. After you float through this logic, you should be able to identify the color of each parachute. Color each one appropriately.

Facts:
1. The turquoise parachute is higher than the orange one but lower than the green one.
2. Purple and red are at the exact same height.
3. The blue parachute and the orange parachute are the highest and the lowest.
4. The purple parachute is directly above the green one.

Tournament Trouble

Talk about tournament trouble! Whew! Natalie was in charge of keeping track of the local tennis tournament results. She got so wrapped up in the game that she did not do her job. Now the tournament is over, but the brackets are empty. Use the facts to see if you can help her put the appropriate names in the appropriate places. (Note...for this particular puzzle, there is more than one correct answer.)

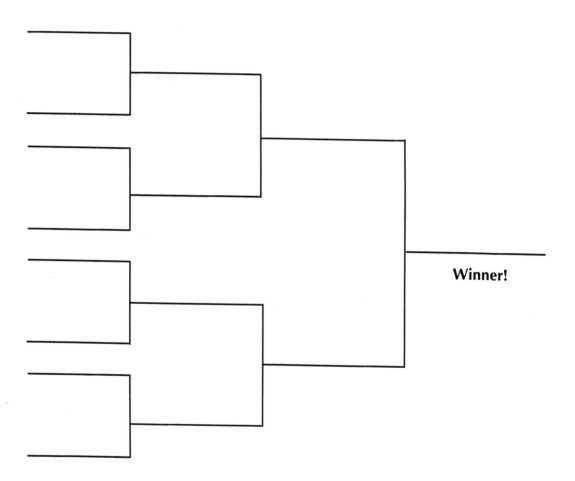

Winner!

Facts:
1. Bryson beat Alex but lost to Himali.
2. During two matches in the first round of the tournament, Andrew lost to Himali, and Alan was defeated by Erica.
3. Himali lost to Caitlin in one of the games.
4. Caitlin defeated Jessica in round 1.

Hang Ten!

Six friends from Santee, California, started off their summer with a splash! They went surfing together. Wade through these statements and figure out which surfboard is which color. There are two hot pink, two purple, one yellow, and one turquoise. Your puzzle will not be complete until you have colored all surfboards appropriately.

Facts:
1. The hot pink boards are not next to each other, but the purple ones are.
2. Yellow is in front of a hot pink board.
3. Turquoise is on the far left or the far right.
4. One of the purples is on the far left or the far right.
5. From the surfers' point of view, the turquoise is somewhere to the left of the purple.

Halloween Screams

Corey, Joel, Keith, Amanda, Carrie, Oliver, and Beau spent Halloween evening together trick-or-treating. As the evening darkened, they ended up in more of a line than a large group. Apply some reasoning to the clues below and label each costume with the appropriate student's name.

Facts:
1. Beau is not last, and Joel is not walking single file.
2. Keith and Carrie are side by side.
3. Amanda and Keith have food costumes.
4. Carrie is between the beetle and Oliver.

Leap Frog

Welcome to Mustagapalooza at Flowing Wells Junior High in Tucson, Arizona! Believe it or not, the teachers are playing Leap Frog. Hop through these statements to figure out which teacher is under each of the frog masks. Here is a list of the teachers playing, listed by their first names: Karyn, Phyllis, Darryl, Tom, Ron, Roger, Linda, Jill, and Janet.

Facts:
1. Linda is somewhere behind Jill but somewhere in front of Ron.
2. Ron is somewhere behind Jill; neither of them are being leaped over.
3. Karyn is leaping over Tom. Janet is somewhere behind Roger.
4. Ron is directly in front of Tom.
5. Phyllis is in the air, ready to leap over Roger.
6. Darryl is in the air; he is behind Phyllis but is in front of Karyn.

Bathing Beauties

Seven friends, Malinda, Diane, Chelsie, Shay, Courtney, Beth and Rachel (all beauties), went to the mall to buy new bathing suits for Memorial Day Weekend. Each bought a different style. Your job is to unravel the facts and label each girl with the correct name. You can do that by deducing who wore which suit!

Facts:
1. Malinda is between the bikini wearer and Rachel.
2. Diane and Chelsie are each standing next to only one other person.
3. Shay is between the sunshine suit and Courtney.
4. From your point of view, Rachel is directly left of Diane.

Up, Down, Round, and Around

The Golding family went to a carnival called Spring Fling. They rode this really cool Ferris wheel. It had small seats, so only one family member rode in each car. Mom, Dad, Grandma, Uncle Joe, twin boys, and twin girls rode the Ferris wheel at the same time. Go round and round through these statements and figure out who is in which car.

Facts:
1. The twin girls are next to each other; the twin boys have one person between them.
2. Mom and Dad are not together, but each of them is next to a different twin girl, and dad is also by one of the twin boys.
3. Uncle Joe is the lowest in this picture, and Grandma is directly opposite Dad.
4. Grandma is between one of the boys and mom.
5. If the Ferris wheel goes clockwise, mom will get off the ride after the twin girls.
6. One twin is opposite Uncle Joe.

Hair Scare!

YIKES! I've heard of bad hair days, but this is ridiculous! Take a look at Billy's aunts. You will not know which aunt is which until you brush up on your logic skills by combing through the facts. As you figure out who is who, be certain to label the hair styles with the name of the appropriate aunt.

The aunts are Michele, Lori, Rayette, Michele, Andrea, Brenda, Helen, Ruthie, and Susie.

1. Michele is not wearing a beehive or a perm.
2. Lori is beside Rayette and Debbie.
3. Andrea is behind Brenda and the permed-hair wearer.
4. Helen is beside the bald person and Ruthie.
5. Susie is behind Michele and Debbie.

Tip of the Hat

$39.00

$45.00

In this next section of the book, you will see puzzles like this, in which you need to calculate the missing prices. The puzzles do increase in difficulty, and some may even seem as if they are not solvable, but they are. Take your time and try several different strategies. It also helps to work with a friend and discuss your thinking.

Example: Look at the puzzle above. Fact: Two baseball hats and one cowboy hat cost $39.00 Fact: *Three* cowboy hats cost $45.00.

Thinking: There are two ways to solve the puzzle of how much a cowboy hat costs and how much a baseball hat costs. One way is to divide $45 dollars by three hats, because you know three hats cost $45. Now you should be able to calculate the cost of the baseball hats.

The second way is to subtract $39 from $45. You will get a difference of $6. That means there is a $6 difference between two baseball hats and two cowboy hats. This means there is a $3 difference between one baseball hat and one cowboy hat. It should be obvious that the cowboy hat is $3 more than the baseball hat, and with this information, you can solve the puzzle. This strategy is a bit more difficult, but practice it with the easier puzzles, and it should help you solve the more difficult ones.

Prices: cowboy hat $_____

             baseball hat $_____

Yum Yum!

See if you can lick this puzzle. You need to use problem solving to calculate the cost of the ice cream cone, the hot dog, and the chips. Then figure out how much the items in row two would cost.

$2.75

$2.75

$3.00

Prices:

= $_____   = $_____   = $_____

Chips 'n' Dip

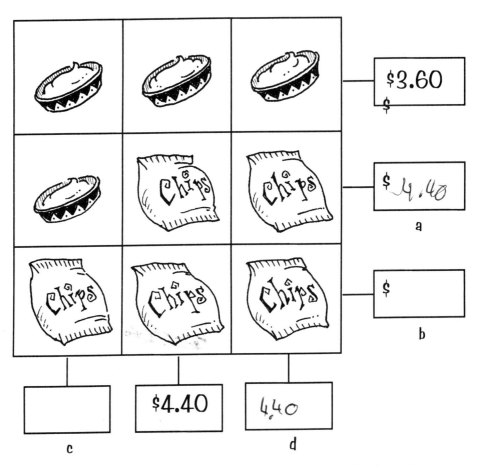

Row prices:
- $3.60
- $ 4.40 (a)
- $ (b)

Column prices:
- (blank) (c)
- $4.40
- 4.40 (d)

Oh, no! Here we go again! Dip into your brain and patience to calculate the missing prices for each row and column. In order to do that, you will have to calculate the individual prices of the chips and dip. Look at every row and every column until you find one that gives you useful information. You can do it!

dip = $_____

chips = $_____

You're Driving Me Nutty!

Don't go nutty trying to solve this puzzle. Just take your time and use logic. Try several strategies, and remember to discuss your thinking with another person. Many times in problem solving...two nuts are better than one!

PRICES:

1 LB. PIÑON NUTS _____

1 LB. PISTACHIOS _____

School Supplies

There is more to getting ready for school than just having the right supplies; you also need to get your brain functioning. You can do that by using logic and problem solving to calculate the cost of these school supplies. If you get stuck, it might help to look back at the puzzle "Tip of the Hat" and read the examples again.

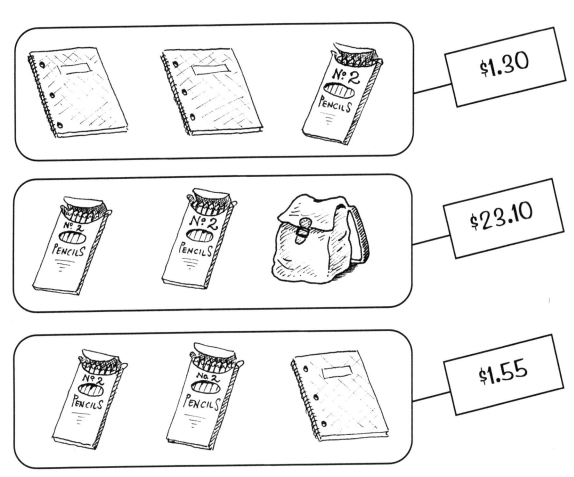

Prices:

Notebook $_____

Pencil Set $_____

Backpack $_____

I'd Like S'More, Please . . .

If you can calculate these prices, you deserve a snack! Take your time and look at every row and column. Compare and contrast and use your brain.

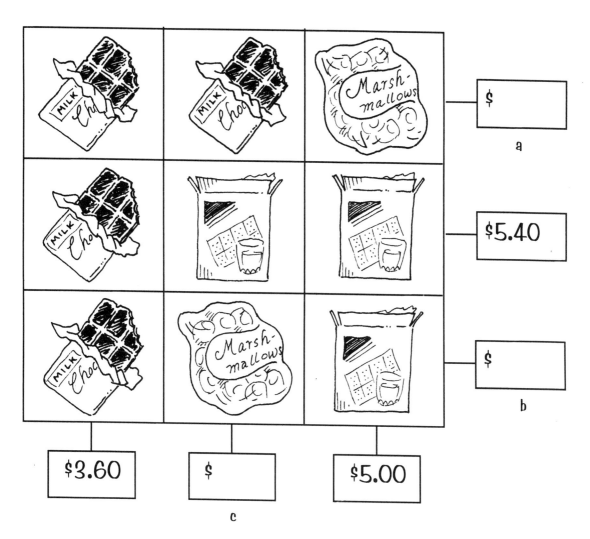

a

$5.40

$ b

$3.60 $ $5.00

c

Prices:

Big Chocolate Bar $_____

Marshmallows $_____

Graham Crackers $_____

Thirst Quenchers

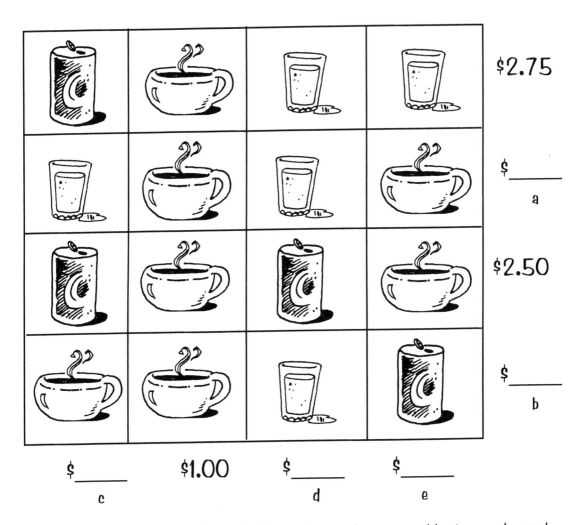

Nothing quenches my thirst for a challenge better than a good logic puzzle, and this is one of those puzzles. Carefully examine each row and vertical column. Pay attention to what you know and what you need to know, and calculate the missing prices. It may take a bit, so you might want to fix yourself something cold to drink.

Prices:

Cola $_____

Juice $_____

Coffee $_____

40   IF2730 Logic Fun

Snack Time

Pete and Leslie are out for a midnight snack. They each want to eat three items but need help calculating the prices of the combinations. Can you help?

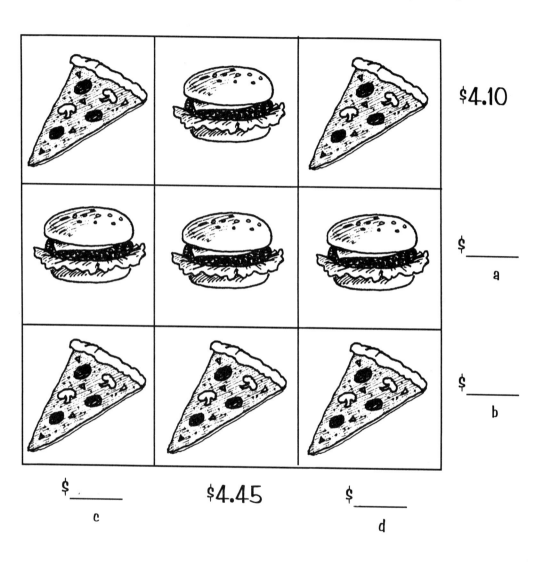

$4.10

$_____
a

$_____
b

$_____
c

$4.45

$_____
d

Prices:

Hamburger $_____

Pizza $_____

Crazy Canned Goods

One of the things adults continually try to do is find the best prices, especially on items they buy in big quantities, like canned goods. See if you can open up this mystery by using logic and problem solving to figure out the prices of the canned goods in this picture. Remember to try different methods of problem solving if your first idea does not work!

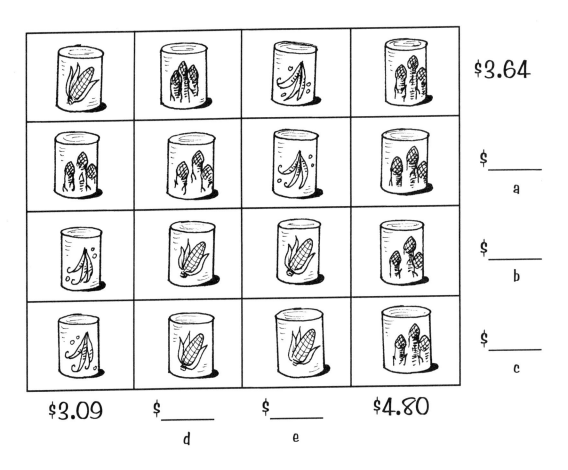

Prices:

Asparagus $_____

Green Beans $_____

Corn $_____

Math Mystery Puzzles

The next section of this book contains puzzles dealing with math. Follow these steps to solve the problems.

Please note that this grid and these clues do not solve a particular puzzle. They are just examples of some of the processes involved.
1. Carefully read the introduction; carefully look at the chart.
2. Go back to the introduction and highlight or underline any specific information. Example: <u>A total of 22 kids ate.</u>
3. Record that information appropriately on the chart.
4. Read the first fact. Decide whether there is specific information that can be recorded at this time; if so, record it. If not, go to the next fact.
5. Continue this process until you have gone over each fact.
6. Now, go back to the first fact and continue, this time checking to see if you can now use the information by cross-referencing. If so, record the new information on the chart.
7. Use addition, subtraction, multiplication, or division, if necessary. Example: Look at the chart below, paying careful attention to what information is given. Suppose a fact tells you that 12 girls ate lunch in the cafeteria. The introduction told you 22 kids ate altogether; now you know 10 boys ate lunch. Record that information.

	Pizza	Salad	Tacos	Total
Boys				10
Girls				12
Total				22

8. Continue this process until the chart is complete and you have solved the puzzle. Have fun!

Babysitter Jitters

Katie and Jesse were saving money to buy school clothes. They started advertising to baby-sit for people, and they got an incredible response. They baby-sat 20 children last weekend. Use the chart to record the facts you deduce to figure out how many children each of them baby-sat over the weekend.

	Friday	Saturday	Sunday	Total
Katie				
Jessie				
Total				

Facts:
1. The same number of children were baby-sat on Saturday and Sunday.
2. Katie didn't feel well on Friday so she did not baby-sit, but Jesse watched ten children Friday.
3. Katie watched twice as many children on Saturday as Jessie did on Sunday.
4. Jesse watched one child Saturday.

Melon Madness

Tony and Marcos were trying to raise money for a trip to Williamsburg, Virginia. They made a deal with a local farmer, who allowed them to sell melons at the fruit stand and let them keep 60% of the profits. It was melon madness! They sold 60 melons *total!* Use the facts and logic to complete the chart and see how many melons of each type the boys sold last Saturday.

	Watermelon	Cantaloupe	Honeydew	Total
Tony				
Marcos				
Total				

Facts:

1. There were 26 watermelons sold and 24 cantaloupes sold.
2. Marcos sold as many watermelons as Tony sold total melons.
3. Tony did not sell any honeydew, but he did sell four more cantaloupes than Marcos sold honeydew.

It's for You . . .

Uh, oh! Acacia and Mariett are on restrictions again. Their parents cannot believe how many phone calls the girls receive. See if you make a connection between the statements and the logic to complete the chart below. When you have recorded everything, you will know how many calls each girl received last week.

Facts:
1. The girls received the same number of calls on Thursday.
2. Acacia received six more calls total than Mariett, but Mariett received two more than Acacia on Monday.
3. Acacia received as many phone calls on Friday as she did on Wednesday and Thursday combined.
4. On Tuesday, Mariett received half as many calls as she did Monday.
5. Seventeen calls were made Friday.
6. Thursday, Acacia received an equal number of calls as she did on Monday.

	Monday	Tuesday	Wednesday	Thursday	Friday	Total
Acacia			6			
Marriett						28
Totals	14					62

Gone Fishin'

Three fishin' buddies just returned from a week-long trip to the Sea of Cortez. They caught quite a few big ones. When you use logic and mathematics to solve this puzzle, you will know who caught how many of each type of fish. They caught so many that they ended up releasing all except what they could eat.

1. Bartley and Roger caught the same number of dorado
2. Only two fishermen caught grouper, and each caught the same number.
3. If you add the number of cabrilla Skipper caught to the number of grouper Bartley caught, the sum will equal the number of cabrilla Roger caught.
4. A total of 120 fish were caught, and, oddly enough, an equal number of each fish were caught.
5. Skipper did not catch any grouper, but he did catch 20 dorado.
6. Roger caught 58 fish.

	Dorado	Grouper	Cabrilla	Total
Roger				
Skipper				
Bartley				
Total				

Y'all Come Back Now...Ya' Hear?

Four friends went to the 1996 Summer Olympics in Atlanta, Georgia. They could not get enough of that southern hospitality. In addition to collard greens, they had some other favorites. In this puzzle, you will calculate how many servings of each finger-lickin'-good food they had.

Facts:

1. Elly's servings of grits plus her servings of fried okra are equal to the number of servings of boiled peanuts she ate.

2. Coley ate an equal number of servings of each food.

3. If you multiply Madeline's servings of grits by Jerry's boiled peanuts, you will know how many servings of okra Madeline ate.

4. Each person ate an equal number of total servings.

5. Jerry's servings of grits are equal to Madeline's servings of grits times the number of okra servings eaten by Elly.

6. Coley ate seven more servings of grits than Madeline who did not eat any peanuts.

	Boiled Peanuts	Fried Okra	Grits	Totals
Madeline				
Elly				
Jerry		0		
Coley				
Totals				120

Oh Christmas Tree, Oh Christmas Tree

Amanda and Alex were busy selling Christmas trees to raise money for their scout troops. They sold 40 Christmas trees! There were three different types of trees. Using your logic skills, complete the chart below and you will know who sold the most trees and what type sold the best.

Facts:

1. Alex sold half as many Douglas firs as Amanda sold white pines.
2. The same number of white pines and Douglas firs were sold altogether.
3. Alex sold 20 Scotch pines which is 10 times the number of White Pines he sold.
4. Amanda was late to the sale. By the time she arrived, Alex had sold all the Scotch pines.

	Douglas Fur	Scotch Pine	White Pine	Total
Amanda				
Alex				
Total				

Donut Holes

Mr. Wells has math contests in his class every Friday. His motto is "If you know, you get a hole!" Everyone wins at least one donut hole, but last Friday Leslie and Peter cleaned up! Together they won more donut holes than they ever imagined—30 total to be exact! Use your logic skills and munch through some math knowledge to figure out how many and what type of donut holes Peter and Leslie munched on!

Facts:

1. There were 13 glazed holes eaten and 12 chocolate eaten.
2. Leslie did not eat any cinnamon, but she did eat two more chocolate than Peter ate cinnamon.
3. Leslie ate as many total donut holes as Peter ate glazed.

	Cinnamon	Glazed	Chocolate	Total
Peter				
Leslie				
Total				

Follow the Yellow Brick Road!

Hendricks Elementary School drama department was putting on the play *The Wizard of Oz*. The teachers were overwhelmed with hopeful actors and actresses. The four most popular roles were the Scarecrow, Tin Man, Lion, and the Wizard. Thirty students tried out for these roles and one third of those were girls. Use logic and the chart to figure out how many boys and girls tried out for each of the characters.

Facts:

1. The same number of students tried out for Scarecrow and the Wizard.
2. Eight students tried out to be the Tin Man, and four tried out to be the Lion.
3. There was one less girl Wizard than boy Scarecrow.
4. No girls tried out for Tin Man, but two tried out for the Lion.
5. When you divide the number of boy Wizards by girl Lions, you get the number of girls who tried out for the Wizard.

	Scarecrow	Tin Man	Lion	Wizard	Total
Girls					
Boys					
Total					

The Best Darn Sandwich in the World

At the Sausage Deli in Tucson, Arizona, making sandwiches is a family affair. Last night, Steve received a big order from a local radio station. He and the crew stayed late to fill the order of 96 sandwiches. Munch through the facts and use critical thinking to complete the chart to see who made how many of each sandwich.

Facts:
1. Jane and Steve made the same number total sandwiches.
2. Toby did not make any Bismarcks, but the number of Omars he made is a two-digit square number which is less than 20.
3. Steve made four less Omars than Jane.

	Uncle Steve	Toby	Jane	Total
Omars				56
Bismarcks				
Total				

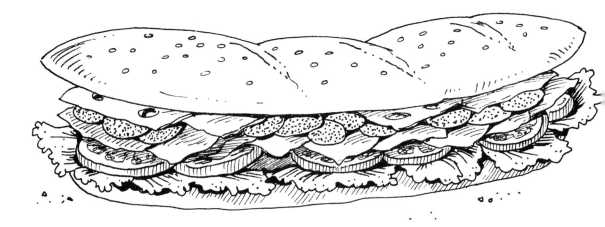

Muffin Mania

Wow! Can you imagine baking 60 batches of muffins? Neither could Mary, Judy, Linda, or Don, until they did last Thursday. They were having a bake sale for the Environmental Awareness Club, and it was muffin mania! When you finish this challenging puzzle, you will know who baked how many and of what type, Here is one hint. There was an equal number of each type muffin baked. Good luck!

Facts:

1. Mary baked eight more banana muffin batches than Linda baked blueberry.
2. Linda baked as many blueberry as Judy baked banana
3. Linda baked two times as many banana as Don baked pumpkin, and Mary baked as many blueberry as Judy baked pumpkin.
4. Judy baked twice as many pumpkin as Linda
5. Mary did not bake any pumpkin, and Judy did not bake banana.
6. Judy baked 12 batches of pumpkin.
7. Mary baked three times as many blueberry batches as Judy did.

	Mary	Judy	Linda	Don	Total
Blueberry					
Pumpkin					
Banana					
Total					

School Spirit Sale!

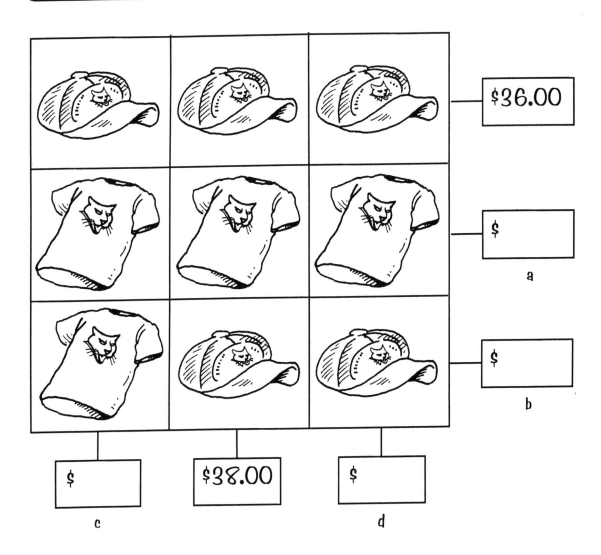

$36.00

$ ____ a

$ ____ b

$ ____ c

$38.00

$ ____ d

With logic and patience, you can calculate the missing prices for each row and column. In order to do that, you will have to calculate the individual prices of the shirt and and the hat. Look at every row and every column until you find one that gives you useful information. You can do it! If you finish early, you can color the hats and shirts to match your school.

Shirt $_____
Hat $_____

Funtastic!

Last Sunday, after church, Chad and Laura went to an amusement park. They had a funtastic time! They did have trouble figuring out how much money they spent on each ride because they bought the tickets in packages. See if you can slide through this mystery by using logic and problem solving to figure out the prices of the individual tickets for the Bumper Boats, Go Carts, and the Water Slide. Remember to try different methods of problem solving if your first idea does not work!
Ticket Prices:

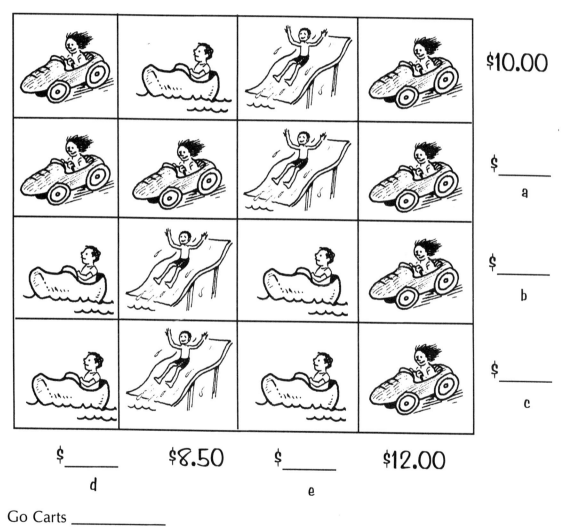

$10.00

$ _____
a

$ _____
b

$ _____
c

$ _____
d

$8.50

$ _____
e

$12.00

Go Carts _____

Water Slide _____

Bumper Boats _____

Answer Key

Fruit Salad — page 3

1. Elizabeth did not bring the pineapple.
2. Carrie is not the youngest.
   Carrie's last name is not McKethen
   Carrie did not bring Kiwi.
   Kiwi is older than at least two persons.
   McKethen did not bring Kiwi.
3. Barnes is not the oldest
   Barnes is not the youngest.
   Barnes did not bring bananas.
   Barnes did not bring watermelon.
   Barnes is not the uncle.
   Others:
   The uncle brought watermelon.
   The banana bringer is younger than the uncle.
   The uncle is not the youngest.

Winter Wonderland — page 4

	Skiing	Snowman	Ice Skating	Sledding
Beth	X			
Josh				X
Damien			X	
Anthony		X		

Bagel Bakery — page 5

	Onion	Sesame	Whole Wheat	Garlic
Tammy		X		
Darryl			X	
Jennifer				X
Josh, the dog	X			

Bottoms Up! — page 6

	Pineapple	Apple	Cinnamon/Struesal	Pineapple/Cherry
Jean		X		
Sue			X	
Minnie	X			
Jodi				X

Rollin', Rollin', Rollin' — page 7

	Bicycle	Tricycle	Unicycle	Rollerblades
Andrea			X	
Seth	X			
Heide		X		
Jason				X

Shell Seekers — page 8

	Conch	Cone	Razor	Oyster	Mollusk
Joshua			X		
Caleb	X				
Kandy				X	
Lucas					X
Randy		X			

Top Dogs — page 9

	Relish	Mustard	Mustard/Onion	Ketchup	Ketchup/Mustard	Ketchup/onion
Matthew				X		
Samuel			X			
Derrick	X					
Mitchel					X	
Bob		X				
Betty						X

Goosebumps — page 10

	nails on chalkboard	howling	cobwebs	cockroaches	screams	darkness	thunder
Tiffany						X	
Gabriel	X						
Jennifer				X			
Laura			X				
Melissa							X
Kyle					X		
Mia		X					

Fraction Action — page 11

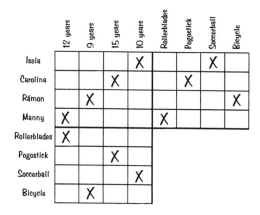

	⅓	7/20	⅝	⅘	.375	.26	.35	.125
Joanna			X		X			
Alex	X							X
David				X		X		
Lydian		X					X	
.26				X				
.35		X						
.125	X							
.375			X					

No Way, José — page 12

	12 years	9 years	15 years	10 years	Rollerblades	Pogostick	Soccerball	Bicycle
Isela				X			X	
Carolina			X			X		
Rámon		X						X
Manny	X				X			
Rollerblades	X							
Pogostick			X					
Soccerball				X				
Bicycle		X						

We Be Jammin' — page 13

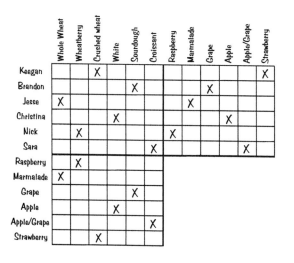

	Whole Wheat	Wheatberry	Crushed wheat	White	Sourdough	Croissant	Raspberry	Marmalade	Grape	Apple	Apple/Grape	Strawberry
Keegan			X									X
Brandon					X			X				
Jesse	X						X					
Christina			X						X			
Nick		X					X					
Sara						X					X	
Raspberry		X										
Marmalade	X											
Grape					X							
Apple			X									
Apple/Grape						X						
Strawberry			X									

Church Camp — page 14

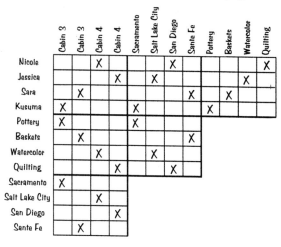

	Cabin 3	Cabin 3	Cabin 4	Cabin 4	Sacramento	Salt Lake City	San Diego	Sante Fe	Pottery	Baskets	Watercolor	Quilting
Nicole			X				X					X
Jessica				X				X			X	
Sara		X				X				X		
Kusuma	X				X				X			
Pottery	X				X							
Baskets		X				X						
Watercolor				X				X				
Quilting			X				X					
Sacramento	X											
Salt Lake City		X										
San Diego			X									
Sante Fe				X								

Cheese, Please — page 15

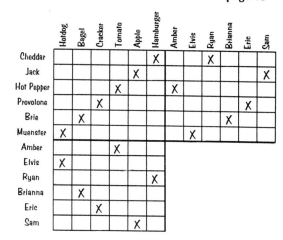

	Hotdog	Bagel	Cracker	Tomato	Apple	Hamburger	Amber	Elvis	Ryan	Brianna	Eric	Sam
Cheddar						X			X			
Jack				X								X
Hot Pepper	X							X				
Provolone			X								X	
Brie		X								X		
Muenster				X			X					
Amber				X								
Elvis	X											
Ryan						X						
Brianna		X										
Eric			X									
Sam					X							

Hang On, Harry! — page 16

				highest elevation			top speed			longest drop		
	Ohio	Florida	California	415 feet	145 feet	132.6 feet	60 mph	100 mph	61 mph	131 feet	137 feet	415 feet
Montu		X				X			X	X		
Mantis	X				X		X				X	
Superman			X	X				X				X
longest drop — 131 feet		X				X			X			
longest drop — 137 feet	X				X		X					
longest drop — 415 feet			X	X				X				
top speed — 60 mph	X				X							
top speed — 100 mph			X	X								
top speed — 61 mph		X				X						
highest elevation — 415 feet			X									
highest elevation — 145 feet	X											
highest elevation — 132.6 feet		X										

The Pancake Mistake
page 18

	Apple cinnamon	Pecan	Banana Nut	Blueberry	Cinnamon	21 years	8 years	16 years	15 years	12 years	23 pancakes	21 pancakes	19 pancakes	18 pancakes	14 pancakes
Daniel		X				X							X		
Annie	X									X		X			
Luna			X						X						X
Niko				X										X	
Michael			X					X			X				
23 pancakes		X						X							
21 pancakes		X				X									
19 pancakes	X								X						
18 pancakes					X			X							
14 pancakes			X						X						
21 years		X													
8 years					X										
16 years			X												
15 years				X											
12 years	X														

Time Out!
page 20

	Black	Schreiner	Valenzuela	Jehle	Abrahms	Krompasky	Renate	John	Manny	Debbie	Linda	Eric
Go carts				X								X
Rollerblades			X								X	
Bungee jumping					X	X						
Water slides	X							X				
Skydiving		X								X		
Scuba diving			X						X			
Renate						X						
John	X											
Manny			X									
Debbie		X										
Linda			X									
Eric					X							

Bats Are Where It's At
page 21

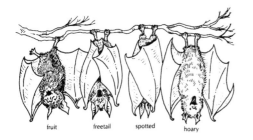

fruit   freetail   spotted   hoary

Summer Snooze
page 22

Jeepers, Creepers!
Where'd You Get Those Peepers?
page 23

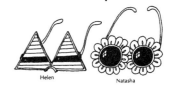

Totally Tubular
page 24

Windy 500
page 25

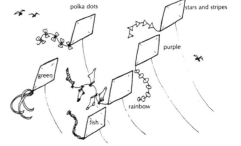

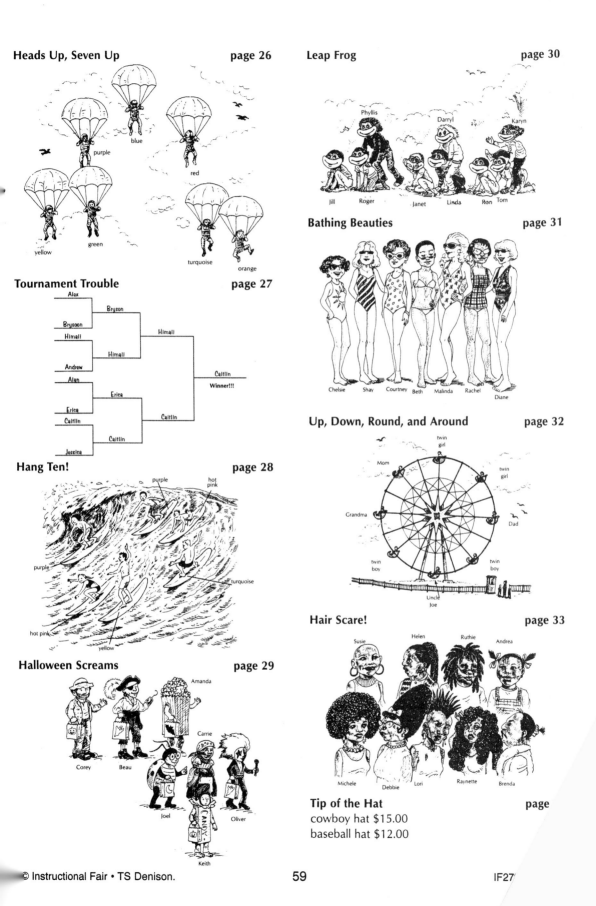

Heads Up, Seven Up
page 26

blue
purple
red
yellow
green
turquoise
orange

Tournament Trouble
page 27

Alex
Bryson
Bryson
Himali
Himali
Andrew
Himali
Alan
Caitlin
Erica
Winner!!!
Erica
Caitlin
Caitlin
Caitlin
Jessica

Hang Ten!
page 28

purple
hot pink
purple
turquoise
hot pink
yellow

Halloween Screams
page 29

Amanda
Carrie
Corey
Beau
Joel
Oliver
Keith

Leap Frog
page 30

Phyllis
Darryl
Karyn
Jill
Roger
Janet
Linda
Ron
Tom

Bathing Beauties
page 31

Chelsie
Shay
Courtney
Beth
Malinda
Rachel
Diane

Up, Down, Round, and Around
page 32

twin girl
Mom
twin girl
Grandma
Dad
twin boy
twin boy
Uncle Joe

Hair Scare!
page 33

Susie
Helen
Ruthie
Andrea
Michele
Debbie
Lori
Raynette
Brenda

Tip of the Hat
page
cowboy hat $15.00
baseball hat $12.00